The Do-Over

_____ poems

Kathleen Ossip

Sarabande  Books

LOUISVILLE, KENTUCKY

Managing Editor
Sarabande Books, Inc.
2234 Dundee Road, Suite 200
Louisville, KY 40205

Library of Congress Cataloging-in-Publication Data

Ossip, Kathleen.
  [Poems. Selections]
  The Do-over : poems / Kathleen Ossip. – First edition.
      pages ; cm
  ISBN 978-1-936747-96-2 (pbk. : acid-free paper) – ISBN 978-1-936747-98-6 (ebook)
  I. Title.
  PS3615.S6A6 2015
  811'.6–dc23

                    2014010250

Cover by Kristen Radtke.
Interior by Kirkby Gann Tittle.
Manufactured in Canada.
This book is printed on acid-free paper.
Sarabande Books is a nonprofit literary organization.

The Kentucky Arts Council, the state arts agency, supports Sarabande Books with state
tax dollars and federal funding from the National Endowment for the Arts.

This project is supported in part by an award from the National Endowment for the
Arts.

Contents

Acknowledgments

Thank you to the editors of these journals, which first published some of the poems:

Boston Review, The Literary Review, Academy of American Poets Poem-A-Day, American Poetry Review, Absent, jubilat, The Awl, Fence, The Atlas Review, Poetry, Court Green, 1913: A Journal of Forms, At Length, MoonLit, A Public Space, Plume, The Hat, StoryQuarterly, TriQuarterly, Magma, The Believer.

"How can we know the journey from the path?" is for Roddy Lumsden; it was written for his Subterranean Homesick Blues Project reading, which took place in New York on October 30, 2009.

"Three True Stories" is for David Trinidad.

"The Millipede" is for Ellen Sauer, Christian Sauer, Muriel Ossip, and Keira DiNuzzo.

Thank you also to Joelle Biele, Christina Davis, Barbara Fischer, Jenny Goodrich, Joe Harrington, Joe Salvatore, Leah Souffrant, Arthur Vogelsang, and Susan Wheeler for encouragement and advice; to the women of the Poet-moms listserv for wisdom, laughs, and handholding; to Kathleen D. Marshall and the staff at the Sylvia Plath archive in the Lilly Library, Indiana University Bloomington; and to the Corporation of Yaddo and Preston Browning at Wellspring House, where I was given time to write some of the poems. Tons of gratitude to the Sarabande team: Sarah Gorham, Kirby Gann, and Kristen Radtke. Thanks and love to Robert Ossip, Muriel Ossip, Al Ossip, and Philip and Ann DiNuzzo.

For Andrea Forster Ossip (1944–2008)
Andy was my stepmother-in-law.

Dimension means nothing to the senses, and all we are left with is a troubled sense of immensity.

—Charles Dutton, early Grand Canyon geologist

Death is not what you think it is; it's actually what I think it is.

—Mark Waldron

1

A. *in May*

Alfresco on a chairbed the woman confirms the natural.
Natural it is to be disgusted and hopeless.
Disgusted and hopeless at being related to her,
Relating to her is what keeps me alive.
Even the unfair trees and the lawn are alive.
Alive with beating life she flies in the face of
Five w's: what when where why why?
On the chairbed she is breaking out of the sun and the lawn.
Really, out of the sun and the lawn and the trees and me. I am
Still studying, aren't you? Whether we accept
These processes or are repulsed by them, we are still studying,
Each of us one cell in a universe of process.
Realm of the universe, hers, and realm of the bourgeois dah-dah-dah.
On the chairbed, in the sun, she's turning yellow.
She's part of the carbon cycle. I toe several pits on the lawn.
She's been eating cherries and has dropped pits on the lawn.
It's natural to have lost my breath and found several
Pits on the lawn.

Mother's Day

I had no mother, I required none.

I believed in mothers like I believed in the pyramids.

They were complicated too. Monumental but hollow. Dusty but beautiful.
Mathematical and confusing. Birth, I believed,

was the brilliant upheaval. Now I see Death is another.

When I think of mother,

you are the image I think of, like a sun. I mean that

I'm not supposed to make friends in a poem, which should be mathematical
and confusing. You are not my mother. I required none. You are a friend who
couldn't help but mother

and now a mass blocks the sun. I want to take your kindness and put it in my hair.

The image is dead! Long live the sensation.

"I'm afraid of death"

I'm afraid of death
because it inflates
the definition
of what a person
is, or love, until
they become the same,
love, the beloved,
immaterial.

I'm afraid of death
because it invents
a different kind of
time, a stopped clock
that can't be reset,
only repurchased,
an antiquity.

I'm afraid of death,
the magician who
makes vanish and who
makes odd things appear
in odd places—your
name engraves itself
on a stranger's chest
in letters of char.

Ode

I sing of a most beautiful man in a factory in Longhua. Fifteen hours he sails among the never-finished piecework, his voice winding in rhythms and phrase groups, sumptuously so. Through the gold-blue day, through the edgy night, his tempestuous mind, the planes of his face amplify Plato. He returns to the dormitory, solitary among many, which makes him beautiful.

•

If I can create the man,
Beauty can't redeem
the iPod nano
made in a five-story factory
secured by police officers.

•

Or an ode to flowers, borne in pairs on threadlike stalks.
Ode to a pond, a pool.
To a willow pattern on her good plates.

•

If she were well and in Longhua
and in the factory and thrown together with him
and they shared a meal and she spoke Cantonese

or he spoke English and overcame
his desolation and distrust
she would befriend the man.

•

The man tries to make a point, a new point, his own point. But no boss wants
that. They only want points they already know, or just quick flowing motion, no
points at all.

•

Healthy is probably the word we use most.
The voice sounds heedful, over-ovened—rhetoric on a scooter.
Extend the dots: griefshock by Xmas.

•

Ode to the container and the thing contained.
Ode to a well-lit room.
Ode to a pearl ring on a warm, fat finger.
Ode to the outskirts of never.
May this ode assert nothing.

•

In a sleep state she is aware of many persons in her: one a cruel dominating man, one an embryo, one Jesus, one a charming flirtatious girl without care, etc.

•

In this expanse, a governance powders, fragile. I'm a cipher, he said, but his friend didn't know what "cipher" meant. On the silent video, a balladeer shatters human dignity.

•

In the dark of the year, the holly wind-holdy, thoughts were and are.

•

The beautiful man is a well. The beautiful man is a mirror. The beautiful man is a valve. The beautiful man is a plug and socket,

it being impossible.

    The man becomes a travelogue, death a bonus gift if you act now, love a regiment of twinges,

it being impossible.

•

He is stately and elaborate and speaks for himself, without any music at all.

•

Ode to a bentwood chair
Ode to discomfort of all sorts
Ode to passivity
Ode to his lightweight jacket
Ode to bad moods and their justification
Ode to the inescapable
Ode to logical transitions, strained and frayed
Ode to the giantess Boredom
Ode to a long regret
Ode to radiation *and* chemo
Ode to the goldsmith bending bracelets for her
Ode to Chanukah *and* the Moon Festival
Ode to limitless compassion

•

This ode's my grinding wheel. When is the last I see of her two-handed. I sit with hands folded, by a pond, a pool, wimpled by unknowing. The beautiful man beside me. Or will see her in shortgrass, summerly.

Tool Moan

I sat at a table outside an Irish pub, with a child I adored and a man I didn't, in a resort town in summer.

Another man sat on a folding chair attempting to entertain the diners with accordion music. At first I wondered if he was a street person, so shabby was he. I heard the waitresses call him Tool Moan.

How delicious, I thought. The accordion equals the tool, the music equals the moan? Above, on the plaza,

a band (lead guitar, rhythm guitar, bass, drums) played, loudly, a funk version of Jimi Hendrix's "Voodoo Child." I wished I could hear the accordion music above the noise

but I couldn't. Before we left home,

my mother had asked, as dinner conversation, "Are we moving through time or is time moving around us?" "I think we're moving through time, Mom"—I was full of my own agency.

Actually time falls on us like a fine rain, almost unnoticed, soaking us to the bone.

Accordion music is the saddest music on earth: agree or disagree? I disagree.

Accordion music is delicate, like the feathers of snow on the mountains that surrounded the town.

The man paid the bill. The child ran ahead. Delicate equals subject to damage (and almost equals Celtic). "You have some competition tonight," I said to Tool Moan as we left.

"I know," he said. Later, back in the hotel room, I realized I'd misheard. His name was Tout le Monde (equals everybody in French). . . .

The Road Trip and the Apron String

Why so fierce! This reaction to her knees,
important as Rushmore.
Let me explicate, I begin. Then I spit.

A spurt of attention yields up
me and Keats, iris to iris. Oh
World of Grownups, tense and shiny, give me a hot rub.

The cornfields are a scourge.
The lung of the country browns.
The bladder fills with droplets.
The measures load with notes.
The songs are all a pleasure and one day

we won't have the pleasure of breathing.

A flare of temper, wonderful and true,
yields up *Have I told you lately*, then *She will not die*.
Dear   , rescue her

or she won't be rescued.
Her breath a flint. Born to the lifespan of a wasp.

Lyric

1.

Squirrels are eating my porch   it's their world too

I call the exterminator

Every day brings filthy compromise

//

I call the vet   the cat's old enough to be neutered

     (Just because I'm bigger than he is
     Even though he didn't ask me to take him home
     Rarely do the small and mute have things the way they want them)

Everyone's tired of my patience   my turmoil has carried me this far

EVERY DAY BRINGS FILTHY COMPROMISE

//

When I look a cow or pig in the eyes, I see a person
I don't feel that way about salmon

I have kept I have lost   my religious faith   I'm eating a salmon

The salmon died in terror and agony   I'm eating him with a vinegar sauce

//

You'll like what you are told to like

This we call the reality effect

So many I could love and do not   so many I could kill and do not

And walk through the world wearing this white face

          (w/moisturizer serums & mascara)

//

I don't know anything I observe so closely I haven't lived

I thought I knew death what did I know

Sylvia and Anne thought they knew death they didn't know anything

      (Didn't know they were going to die anyway?)

//

Her body one long tube with an overgrowth in the middle

My friend to be even one more day with you.

//

(Every day brings filthy compromise.)

//

I came from salt water   in August I swim in salt water

Cancer is my default horror

Fear is not the way for me now I need something bigger?

There's a crowd of people and animals heading westward on the run
There's a pack of beasts and people heading westward on the run
Powerless under the moon   powerless under the sun

2.

Meaning is made—Wonder has no shade

(Says a placard partway down the Grand Canyon)

These dark days the clouds hide the sun.

                                        Gravity's a bright snare

                        (Say I, standing on the edge of the North Rim)

                                        To keep us locked here.

3.

At the mouth of the ravine   (we are home now)
                                        the Weckquaesgeeks camped

They fished swam collected oysters and clamshells planted corn and possibly
    tobacco

                        We walk every day through a haunted house

//

Dear values absurd chaotic and tight,

I never want to forget how this feels   I will of course forget

//

Dear values absurd chaotic and tight,

Appraisal makes me nervous   aggression makes me mad   is true

The reality effect is true

Her body one long tube with an overgrowth in the middle is true

I can stare and stare and still not see it   (truth)   is true

My life is true   my death is true   the ravine is true

//

I wouldn't pay slave wages   I wouldn't sit down and have lunch with
THEWOMANWHOCLEANS"MY"HOUSE

                                    without checking my texts

Modesty kindness humility acceptance   these too are genius

                                    the kinds we need now

CALM DOWN YOU'RE NOT AS SMART AS YOU THINK YOU ARE

//

This one has no soul and that one has no soul   Death is OK for some

In the summer of economic collapse   in the summer of widespread famine

(can't bear to look back   have done that in last book)

                              I execute   I exfoliate   I Gothicize

//

What caused the economic collapse   me so feckless and dreamy

I've been irresponsible   I have no pension   I will die in poverty

I'm a poetess   I'll be killed and eaten   I have no money

I make a beeline for the essential   I think I'm so great

(Ultimate putdown of my childhood   "She thinks she's so great.")

I ride a zipline over the ravine it's great

//

Dear values absurd chaotic and tight,

I think I'm so great to avoid losing light

I sit on the banks of the river   the bodies of my enemies float by

(Death is OK for some)

salmon   Weckquaesgeeks   children I'm oblivious of

//

I don't want much   I want   at my best   to be most loved

At my most ambitious to be most coddled

I want to be oblivious and kind

I want to be rich and humble

I want to believe in reincarnation   an eternity of do-overs

                                                            and because I want to

I find the hidden sun:

                    There's a crazy bright object stapled to the Western sky
                        There's a crown of fire bragging in the Western sky
                        I'll brag right along with it   I am never gonna die

2

Ghost Moon

This is the light of the culture: gold and misleading.
The moon of the culture is full; its light is thick.
The moon is famous, I've read it smells like gunpowder.
The moon binds the town in ivory plastic wrap.
The streetlight does not even bother to shine tonight.
Only once a month is the moon so bright, so bright!
I absorb its rays, I'm sure they do my skin good.

The moon is no drug. It is a voyeur
Clicking the same porn links over and over.
Or—no, wait, that's me. The moon
Is that white disk up there, most definitely.
Most definitely it is poached or steamed
in a black broth of quietness. I eat here.
I make beds here. Here I stare at screens.

The moon is manic, it has a coin-like shape.
My eyes spiral with inattention.
The Lord God Yehovah is as vengeful as the moon,
The Goddess Devi is as nurturing.
How I, on the sidewalk in front of the dry cleaner's,
would like to believe in the moon.
Or—no, wait, how I would like the moon to believe in me.

Oh. I seem to be crying. I am overstimulated.
The moon binds the bank in ivory plastic wrap.
Inside the bank, the boxes are all empty,
mournful in the after-business hours.
They mourn for the jewelry and certificates that have vanished.
The moon sees all, the moon is seen from everywhere.
And the message of the ghost moon: I'm vast, you're vast, we've been done.

How can we know the journey from the path?

Keep a clean nose
Watch the plain clothes
— Bob Dylan

A tumbleweed bounces by
the institutions of power
and the institutions of power or
the daisies in front of the institutions of power

are my last big chance at a voice.
A tumbleweed bounces by.
Am I morally obligated to care for this organism
or can I kill it? I'm loving my

desperate organism.
Talking in class was "pretty cool" at one time,
my last big chance at a voice. I wanted to
go play bingo and breakfast at IHOP.

Now, everything's not OK.
Everything's *not* OK. Heavenly daisies,
though. Mary Queen of Heaven
in the prayerbook

bare toes crushing the serpent
looked silly. And the institutions of power
look silly if you're from them in-
sulated enough. They're losing their suits

in the institutions of power. Helen
Vendler's looking mighty like Sasha Fierce.
Both have expert memories
of those who appreciate their bitchy science.

The beauty's only part of it.

Perseverance is beautiful, and embarrassing.
How many institutions of power remain?
Several. Several. Organisms are delicate

and bleed.
They bleed
and we are morally obligated to care for them.
How should I know what's right?

Ask a good question:
You'll have success immediately.
I got a flowering plant as a present.
The original flowers and tall attractive leaves

have died, leaving a low, dull mess.
Am I morally obligated to care
for this that shares my home?
My husband is baffled by my spiritual questioning

and my boyfriend is irritated by my spiritual questioning
and my girlfriend ignores my spiritual questioning
and my boss fears my spiritual questioning
and I'm loving my desperate organism

and my last big chance at a voice

On Political Crisis

~~Grace~~ Success consists in ignoring
what you don't like, as a bunny

leaps past tinfoil
in his search for greens.

You don't need spring fever
in a garden of tinfoil;

to seize the choice bit
in place of the glittering

or the made-up
means the whole plot

will be changed, gladly.
In the vicinity,

all relish posturings;
the problem is how to remain chaste

next to so many furry bodies
when those we thought would cuddle us,

whether weeping or jeering,
have fled.

The problem is how to *remain*.
Words are no doorstep whatsoever

for the orphaned and penniless.
The hop to the shed

is driven by wanting
to fill the wreck with ~~delights~~ reordering.

The Great Man is dead,

and no, we don't shimmer on the shattered green. I rebuke all indictment,
I rebuke every indictment, I want only the clear light. And no, I don't mean
Broad Daylight, Inc. but bare attention to the frolic and detour of the human
imagination, an appetite for peace, the sweet do-nothing. Didn't he

kind of pose and embrace the past, didn't he wear underpants and a tank top,
wasn't he feminine, really? We used to prepare calm answers to his questions,
trying to rid ourselves of the flat *a* in *Daddy*. His ear appeal! His permission,
restriction, attribution! All of equal weight and nativeness. And that was the
mystery of the crisis: how a *good guy* (the hype description) never could see the
clear light.

Where tulips solace and pass away, he's bequeathed a fine night, fine morning.
In the cemetery, living things nip at the no-can-do. Mice study their habits over
and over. The guests never can hear the music. Their expressions make such a
fuss with very little—a grayish sky like a ghost before the storm, the economy
drifting through—

Do we wait for a plain statement of theme? Do we leave, shocked, the vigil?

January 20, 2009

It's hard to keep identities

from ruination—if they're not in writing, it's impossible. In an age so primal I
fell in love with him, we were accused of lacking a sense of humor. A bit too
regressive for me, a Great Man! Who had a god in him. Who reappeared so
faithfully in his bed, we could have been buried together in the same grave.
His NO gets pasted into which scrapbook tonight? Just why should it be
written down, especially if as a result I am the guilty one. Shining brass on the
hearth bangs out a shame and wonder

so great I fall in love with him
and will never see him again
but was with him last Christmas.

He listened

to my heartbeat all night. There is no point of intersection. There is
consolation in language (*for rest or foreplay*); but out of it, static repetitious
neural circuits. I tell you, he mounted and turned the peg this way and
that way, with seven payoffs, seven times. It was fun. Understanding the
arrangement

doesn't feel like perfect clarity
(sign of a laxness of ideas or a layer of silt
now washed away like a relationship).

Veterans Day

Las Vegas is the other side of Kabul.
The fanatic is always concealing a secret doubt.

It's not as bad as you think,
making out with a corpse,

the corpse in dress blues.
Let us imagine him as a newborn.

Let us imagine them all as newborns
who see an island and say *Look, it's just over there,*

let's go over there. Let us imagine they swim
to the lagoon and the palm-fringed beaches,

and grow up and drink fruit water and play catch
with a coconut. The handsome boys in khaki

either betray you or they die.
When they die they go to Vegas,

where they are violent and always busy
at the video slots. Each machine must pay back

at least 75% over its lifetime. By law.
Murderousness creates its own market.

A newborn is murderous
but can't do anything about it.

Amy Winehouse

All song is formal, and you
Maybe felt this and decided
You'd be formal too. (The eyeliner, the beehive: formal.)

When a desire to escape becomes formal,
It's dangerous. Then escape requires
Nullity, rather than a walk in the park or a movie.
Eventually, nullity gets harder and
Harder to achieve. After surgery, I had
Opiates. I pushed the button as often as I could.
Understood by music was how I felt. An escape
So complete it became a song. After that,
Elegy's the only necessary form.

Steve Jobs

Say you lost all your money, or turned against your ambition.
Then you would be at peace, or
Else why does the mind punish the body?
Vengeance is mind, says the body.
Ever after, you're a mirror, "silver and exact."

Just like the bug in a string of code, the body defies the mind
Or looks in the mirror of the mind and shudders.
Better instruments are better because they're
Silver*ish* but intact.

Troy Davis

The clock is obdurate,
Random, and definite.
Obdurate the calendar.
You thump on the cot: another signature.

Did it didn't do it would do it again.
And if a *deferred* dream dies? Please sign the petition.
Very good. Let's hunt for a pen.
If you thump, there's another signature and
Signatures are given freely by the signer's hand.

Lucian Freud,

Lingering over
Unlovely bodies,
Couldn't help
Intuitively rendering
A whole
Nother angel.

Facts are
Relics—an
Effect worth
Undertaking: yes,
Dear daylight?

Donna Summer

Discourse that night concerned the warm-blooded love we felt.
On the divan and in the ballroom and on the terrace, we felt it.
Now virtue meant liking the look of the face we lay next to.
Never mind the sting of the winter solstice.
All discourse that night concerned the warm-blooded love we felt.

Something lifted us higher. Her little finger told her so,
Untangling, with careless skill, the flora of the sexual grove.
Master physician with a masterly joy in wrapping up
Mud-spattered, coke-dusted wounds at midnight, when it's too
Early to stop dancing and go home. Our lily-minds soothed by her
Royalty concealed in the synthesizers in the flora of the sexual grove.

Three True Stories

1. Uncle Bob, my mother's brother, was my godfather. My mother has told me that when he was young, he was funny and creative: for example, he slipped coal into her stocking one Christmas Eve; he conceived of a "zapper" that would shut a TV off when the commercials came on (years before the invention of remote controls); he had an elaborate theory about how LBJ was responsible for JFK's murder. But before I was old enough to know him, he got multiple sclerosis, which advanced quickly and severely. In all my memories of him, he is an invalid, uncommunicative and at times combative. By the time I was 12, he was bedridden; he died when I was 35. The night after I went to his funeral, I lay in bed. Right before I fell asleep, I had a waking dream or vision: Uncle Bob walking into the bedroom and kissing me on the forehead (as he never did in life), as if to say "Goodbye. I love you." A tingling shock, a sensation like nothing I'd ever felt before, went through my entire body, and I knew it was a genuine visitation.

2. One night I had dinner at an expensive Manhattan restaurant with a Distinguished White Female Poet, a Soon To Be Distinguished White Male Poet-Critic, and a Venerable White Man of Letters. I talked with Distinguished White Female Poet about having a mother and being a mother. I talked with Soon To Be Distinguished White Male Poet-Critic about raising kids. Venerable White Man of Letters didn't have kids, and I felt bad about leaving him out of the conversation. Later I heard him say to Soon To Be Distinguished White Male Poet-Critic, "You and <name of Already Distinguished White Male Poet-Critic> are the only true poet-critics writing today." When we had left (I of course didn't pay for my dinner) and were trying to get a cab, Distinguished White Female Poet told me, "Go stand on the corner and look blonde."

3. We watched the 2012 Super Bowl because Madonna performed the halftime show: a spectacle that introduced her new single "Give Me All Your Luvin'" with the help of LMFAO, Nicki Minaj, M.I.A., and CeeLo Green, who came out at the end in a black robe, to lead a gospel choir singing backup to my very favorite Madonna song, "Like a Prayer." Over the next month, the new song went straight to number 10 on the charts. Muriel and I loved it, singing along whenever it came on the radio. But after the Super Bowl marketing push faded, it sank fast. Muriel said, "It's a great song, but it should be sung by someone else." "Why?" "Madonna's too old to be singing gimme all your love. It needs to be sung by someone who has more . . ." "More what? Youth?" "Someone who has more time."

The Millipede

We didn't know how to begin, the five of us—
you and I (sisters), my daughter, your son, our niece,
didn't know where to begin in the scrubby woods,
past gas stations and Friendly's and into patchwork shade.

You had promised a hike, a two-hour hike—
on that August afternoon all we could walk,
with the kids, the packs, the bag of clementines,
five half-eaten lunch sandwiches, five canteens.

The map at the trailhead showed a waterfall.
We followed a dry creekbed, rough with pebbles.
The trees would spend, I'd read, 300 years growing,
then 300 years living and 300 dying.

You saw a rotten gray log, a pointed rock:
"Isn't it beautiful?" "No," I laughed. The kids balked
and grumbled. "I mean, I like being out in nature…"
"No, you like being *outside*, as in a chair,"

you reminded me. "Who wants a clemmie? Water?"
Your son ran ahead. The day grew hotter.
The girls wanted him to wait up. We were stuck.
No signs, no guide, our cellphones wouldn't work

and we didn't know how to go on. This was the summer
the economy couldn't grow. "What grows forever?"
was my opinion. I knew a thousand experts
would tell me a thousand times how wrong I was.

The sugar and Vitamin C revived us a little.
We found the waterfall, not more than a trickle
that dry summer. Now to find the trailhead . . .
Three teenage boys on the cliff, smoking weed,

yelled "Look for the footbridge. Once you see it you'll know
you're almost there. Can't miss it." We missed it, though,
like the dumb economy missed, again and again.
Our way was up a perilous incline.

Your son turned over a stone. "Look! Isn't it beautiful?"
A millipede, many-legged, red-brown, immobile.
"Move!" your son said, poking with a stick.
My daughter: "No, don't do that! You'll hurt it."

Our niece said, "A millipede is not a caterpillar."
A millipede doesn't want a do-over.
The millipede didn't move and never flew.
And where was the footbridge? Still we didn't know how

to end. (Much later, we did arrive, unclear:
"We hated it, let's do it again next year."
In the scrubby woods, the millipede thinks *I'm alive
and safe where I am. Why should I move?*)

3

A. *in January*

At the moment, we have moments that breathe or smile.
Never minding about the fly on the fresh-laundered curtain, she
Doesn't want to miss out on anything small—that
Rabbit thinking, in the hungry garden, with its hungry eyes.
Essential strangeness, open your threatening fist
And make friends with her brittle naked skin.

For what is the purpose of judgment, with its snap-snap?
Open your weakening fist, oh Nakedness, and make
Ready to slide across a tundra.
She asks my advice, I shut up.
The most excellent thing you can be is quiet, to grant the
Essential strangeness of a body that has no fixed place,
Resembling a cobweb that marries one violet to another.

On these small things we fix all hope.
So what is the evolutionary point of love and death?
Spiritual growth?, I blab, purpose-headed to the end.
In the essential strangeness of the garden,
Pigeons on the grass, a big mess, no alas.

What is A.

A leather sack time and space

happen above.

Upon death she becomes a fame
fragrant as orange

an honest sentence in English

a hard case
worked out in the end

whose stunning comfort

stapled me.

What is Death

1.

In Hartsdale, home of America's first canine pet cemetery
and the world's first Carvel ice cream store, once home to

the Weckquaesgeeks, sub-tribe of the Algonquins, whose name
means "place of the bark kettle," which kettle appears on the town

seal today, one of the few communities surrounding
New York City that still has two working farms, both on

2.

Secor Road, not far from Homewood Road, where
a window cleaner drips clorox onto her house — she

dies, not at all like Lazarus.
A house full of beloved objects, a house where no dinner party

ends without whipped cream. When death comes it's big
and tastes like the beach. The contractor tells her he can't fix the stain.

3.

Death is something you can add to every day.
The drool spot. Neglect of hair nails teeth.

In the living room: antique marble collection, antique rattle collection, antique
postcard collection, antique rosewood piano, Chinese rug in gold and green,
    stack of

books by friends and family, photographs of friends and family, papier mâché mask
made by her daughter in fourth grade, something you can add to every day.

4.

In Hartsdale, there's a stone in the wheeling snow. Which is the nearest thing to
    wisdom.
Spirit, like an arrow, speeds up when it nears the target.

Her spirit, whisked to the corner, where the audience left it.
Death

a will dissolves. A jump past the dread of severance, a suspension, a caper. No
new purchases now.

5.

My first time in Hartsdale, I thought "This is the nicest house I've ever seen."
The audience quits the spirit,

a door, a wing, a billow, or a slight peeling.
In Hartsdale, there are wood and smelting materials to make nails.

There are hammers and saws and electricity to run them.
There is the Lone Guard who still stands, arms to the side.

6.

In Hartsdale, she is granted a complete passivity.
All observation, like a newborn.

Enter the Neolithic poppy, the gentling poppy
no one has to kick.

Morphine is the prototype narcotic drug and is the standard against which all other
opiates are tested \ like a mother's arms.

7.

Ferncliff Cemetery on Secor Road is famous as the burial grounds for many celebrities
including Aaliyah, Malcolm X, Judy Garland, Jerome Kern, Joan Crawford,

Basil Rathbone, Ed Sullivan, Jam Master Jay, Gerry Mulligan, James Baldwin, Jim
Henson, Tom Carvel, Oscar Hammerstein, Thelonious Monk, and Paul Robeson.

John Lennon was cremated there.
What??!! Above us only sky?

8.

In Hartsdale, we make a jump past the dread of severance.
The Lone Guard lends a pomp.

It doesn't hurt.
There is an awareness of duration,

something you can add to every day.
Recognition is no paltry occurrence.

9.

Above us only sky.
We don't have the tools, yet, to prove

much of anything. I believe in cosmic energy, spirit
heading to reunite with the source while our

bodies burn to ash or decompose. She would say:
Enjoy life on earth because this is all there is

10.

and I can't find the tools to disprove it.
How do you stay in heaven?

Is it a kind of sophisticated rewind?
Are there wood and smelting materials to make nails?

Are there hammers and saws and electricity to run them?
Also, who builds the houses and buildings?

11.

Is there such a thing as paint or are they all just wood-colored?
To create an image of what I mean

only makes it worse.
At some point, construction must end. And repairs.

In Hartsdale, an object of mourning is still an object.
Look, there are stars above us:

12.

foreground out of focus,
background gem-clear.

She is emerging (she has no choice)
into a place

like sex or childbirth,
one thing to the observer, something very different to the participant.

13.

Some people only feel comfortable in one world of definitions.
Some appreciate variety.

Scientists don't describe a star as big or small.
Stars are bright because they're massive and hot.

The Lone Guard protects what? What infinity looks like.
What does infinity look like? It hurts.

14.

Its bodilessness hurts.
We left from Hartsdale, her last summer,

to the beach, the Jersey shore, the last time
at last, where her spirit, trailing an oxygen tank, pinked up a bit,

and her body sat on the beach, a gray day, the last time,
above us only sky   before us the elastic sea.

15.

In Hartsdale, she confides all her secular traditions; also she begins to prioritize voting.
It's no longer possible for anyone to stop where she is.

She wasn't a person for whom ideas were more important than people.
A biography associates bitterness with death: this

is not absolutely bad and not absolutely good. I was told: You need not have a feeling
about everything that happens. And everything can be repaired but.

16.

"But what will it mean for me?" (selfish)
"It's been more than a week, hasn't it?" (confused)

"Are you a little sad?" (best shut up)
Lying on her side like a baby or a stone

Icedrop
into paren(peace)theses.

17.

When you die, you die. Your body
returns to the earth and those living live on until they die too.

Your spirit doesn't float around after you're gone.
Your spirit is nothing more than your conscious and unconscious

thoughts and feelings. When your body dies, your thoughts die too.
This I don't believe or disbelieve.

18.

Hartsdale "is not down in any map, true places never are." (Melville)
In Hartsdale she makes her "effort at conclusion." (Dickinson)

In Hartsdale, her last night, I scrubbed the stove, which had been neglected.
I rubbed her back.

Neither big nor small but massive and cold,
her bright face shone no more.

19.

Though "not down in any map," Hartsdale is a hamlet
and a census-designated place (CDP) located in the town of Greenburgh,

Westchester County, New York. It is full of cemeteries
littered with those who wished themselves permanent.

Nature retains its emotional power (look there are stars above us!)
which hurts.

20.

At some point, nothing more can be built.
The Lone Guard releases the body-spirit

which was beloved in the house that was beloved.
The love grows elastic, something very different to the observer,

the extreme
natural of it, the extreme unnatural.

Sonnet for A.

With what spirit or intention
does your absent breath outsleep
in forlorn believement
when you're all all over?
Whatsoever thy hand findeth to do
isn't hard to master.
The letting go
does not meet my personal ethics,
abandoned sum
transferred into our treasure.
I should not entertain any fear,
as stated by our culture.
A song of love and death makes its own
bitter symmetry, that's the myth of achievement.

Libraries & Museums

Their hush and their order and their devotion to the past are a deep comfort to us.

But silence has a way of making you want to fill it.

More than anything else,

we wanted to hear you sing. To sing yourself into a stroke, if necessary.

In the house we rented for its nearness to libraries and museums,

the dead woman's mother lay beside me in the bed.

This was death at a remove, like a library or a museum.

A sobbing fit, and then,

metaphorically, the cavalry arrives. Suddenly

the house is full to bursting, the trees full to bursting, the fridge full to bursting.

You can't capture a scene like that, not with a phone, not with a camera.

You can't preserve it.

Though we long for the hush, more than anything we want to hear

you sing again in a voice not young.

4

"No use"

On October 21, 1962, Sylvia Plath wrote one poem that became two. The original two-section poem, which she called "Amnesiac," separated when *The New Yorker* accepted one of the sections and not the other.

She was left with the first, rejected section, which was titled "Lyonnesse" by Ted Hughes after her death, and the second, *New-Yorker*-published section, "Amnesiac."

Both poems begin with the same phrase: "No use."

"No use whistling for Lyonnesse!" "No use, no use, now, begging Recognize!"

"Amnesiac" is a rant at Ted Hughes, not at all disguised by her use of the third person. She accuses him of forgetting their life together and abandoning her and their children.

In "Lyonnesse," she accuses God, "the big God," of forgetting the ancient country that bordered Cornwall, which, according to legend, sank into the sea.

"Lyonnesse" continues: "Sea-cold, sea-cold, it certainly is"—a reply to Walter de la Mare's "Sunk Lyonesse" which begins "In sea-cold Lyonesse. . . ."

Thanks to her habit of journal-keeping and her resolve to memorialize her experience in writing, Sylvia forgot nothing.

On March 4, 1963, three weeks after her daughter's suicide, Aurelia Plath wrote an open letter to *The Observer* in London, to "thank the many kind people . . . who helped and befriended" Sylvia.

The letter continues: "Those who systematically and deliberately destroyed her know who they are." Next to this sentence, Aurelia wrote in pencil "A & T"—Assia, the woman for whom Ted Hughes left Sylvia, and Ted.

At the top of the page, Aurelia wrote "Not Sent! No use now!"

This is the difference between *being forgotten* and *trying to forget*. The survivor tries to forget. She can no longer act in the interest of the one who's gone

and my writing this is no use ("No use!" screams the corpse) and not in the interest of you.

Three Short Lyrics

Memory

Go slow go slow go slow go slow,
with full round voice she said.
After her sphere of influence,
what shakes down crazily—

That golden haze of retrospect,
those trees too green for apes.

Morning Phrases

The boy next door or down the street.
Frost on the mouse's corpse, on the leaf.
Pulled off in the boxcar. Grey Goose, neat.

(Sentimentality: defense against mourning: changes bitter to sweet.)

To You, Muse

Snowdrops   spare and small.
Sparrows easy to stare at. Un-   bearableness, what else?
No more truths!   A story, please.
Free verse   spare and small.

After

The first time I met Jen she looked unclean, as if she'd slept in a full face of makeup. She was eating a vegetable sandwich on spelt bread in her office. She was dressed beautifully though, and her coppery hair was long and glossy, and she'd turned off the fluorescent overhead light in her office and brought in a couple of pink-bulbed lamps instead. Only the uncleanness and the sandwich made her at all approachable.

She had transferred from the Los Angeles office. I'd heard she was coming, the new woman in junior management. She was management, I was creative. Unden Books made a big deal about prizing its creatives. We shook hands and said that we were looking forward to working together.

(Creative meant you could read manuscripts and pick out which were good. Management meant you could figure out ways to sell or P&P—package and promote—the good manuscripts.)

She wants power, you want meaning, said my little voice, which might have stood for otherworldliness. But I ignored it. It seemed too harsh, the snobbish judgment of a book-nerd.

"I've been wanting to meet you," Jen said. "I think we have a lot in common."

"Really?" That could only be a compliment, coming from beautifully dressed and tinted junior manager Jen. We were both in our early thirties, but she had been working steadily for Unden for the past seven years, the big payoff being this move to New York. I had knocked around a few different small publishers, advancing (intern, assistant, senior assistant, junior editor, etc.) so subtly my progress was barely noticeable to anyone but me.

"Of course! I've read some of your reports. We like the same books, we have a similar aesthetic. I feel like we're friends already." When she smiled she looked into my eyes good and bright. "Let's have lunch sometime soon."

When we had lunch about a month later, Jen was depressed. She asked me to grab something at the vegan restaurant across 56th Street.

"I'm so depressed."

"You don't seem depressed." She was smiling, she was at work, not in bed, and she'd applied, expertly, lipliner and a peachy lipcream.

"Well, I'm not depressed now, being here with you!" An appealing little high sigh meant that she was ready to talk seriously.

"I'm not *happy*. When they gave me the job in New York, I expected a promotion. You know? The senior management job. Clarissa's old job. She left three months ago. It's just sitting there. And so far, Ted hasn't said one word. I don't feel *appreciated*."

I saw that by depressed she meant not entirely satisfied. She didn't have everything she wanted. She wasn't used to struggle. That was appealing too.

"Jesus, I know you what mean." And even though I hadn't thought of myself as quite so driven, suddenly I did know what she meant. Her drive infected me. "I've been wondering about the senior creative position."

"Oh, really? *Really*. That's interesting. Tell me."

I wanted the job because it paid more. I wanted the job because it would mean I was part of the family at Unden Books. But mostly I wanted the money. And to be part of the family. I couldn't seem to focus on why, but I wanted it.

I thought maybe Jen could be some kind of guide for me, Virgil to my Dante. I had struggled to understand office politics and the sly variations of clothing, posture, eye contact, and shoptalk that paved the way for the successful. I had survived at Unden through quick good work and inoffensiveness, but even I knew there was a limit to how far those could take me.

"I know I'm good at what I do. I have a kind of intuition, I mean I can read two pages and see where a book is going, and know what's going to kind of … interest the market. I have a great track record but it's just been hard to make that next jump into more responsibility. And you know, it'd be terrific to work with you, I think we could make an amazing team. . . ." For a Libra who always saw five sides of any question, I thought I argued my case pretty well. Jen's focus already seemed to be a good influence.

I had packaged and promoted my struggle as ambition. Ambition interested her. I saw interest light her up. Then, as she calculated, the light narrowed to a single point.

"It will take some doing," she said.

"You mean wait until after. . . ."

"The spring launches, yeah."

"Well, I've waited this long. What's a few more months?" Jen's look of distaste might have been directed at a vacuum cleaner without enough suck. "If we're going to be friends you'll have to lose the passive attitude," it said.

"I wish I could talk to my mother about this," she said.

"What do you mean?"

"She died two years ago. She had lung cancer. But up until she got sick, she was always watching over me, helping me with my career. She was a real winner. She knew how to handle people."

"Was she in publishing too?"

"No, she was in marketing research. She was the first woman to head the division at Nestlé USA."

I was impressed. My mother had lived more of a sitcom mom kind of domestic life. "You must miss her," I said. Then, eager to cheer her up: "You deserve that job!"

"We both deserve those jobs!" said Jen.

"They'd be crazy not to give you that job!" I said.

"I like for things to happen organically. But I guess I'll have to make it happen organically." Her smile, soft and breathtakingly focused at the same time. "It all depends on Ted Unden."

The summer I was twenty-two, before I moved to the city, I went on a road trip with a boyfriend to Lily Dale. Lily Dale is a Victorian-era spiritualist community on a pretty lake in the southwestern part of New York State. The spiritualists take up residence for the summer in pastel-painted cottages and offer readings where they claim to put you in touch with loved ones who have died, except they never say died, they say passed over. I was not exactly a believer, but I craved experiences that were magical, transcendent, or otherworldly. Put another way, I had a hard time sustaining an interest in "real life." Dreams, coincidences, $10 tarot readings, and passing encounters with psychotics were my typical fixes, but Lily Dale would be a genuine quest.

Ralph was a stable, placid guy who humored me in my pursuits. I was broke and Ralph was thrifty, so we didn't pay for a private reading, but we went to a couple of the public meetings where the spiritualist would offer messages from the other side to random people in the audience.

The meeting took place in a little paved grove at the edge of the woods. Through the pines we could see the blue lake winking. A wishful audience sat on folding chairs and waited to see if the spiritualist, a plump woman in her forties with a perfunctory haircut dyed sunflower yellow, would single them out. After contemplating us for a while, she pointed to me and asked me to stand up.

"I'm getting a message. From a tall man. A tall man with light hair. A tall slim man."

I couldn't think of anyone that might be.

"He was a professional man. A professional man who wore a suit and tie to work. In an office, he worked in an office. Well-respected. . . . Well-respected in the community?"

My father's Italian family was abundant with short soulful working-class men who lived modest but long lives. My mother's Irish family was full of men who died young of circulatory problems.

I remembered a sepia photo of a farm league baseball team. My mother's father was in the group shot. He was tall and slim and I guessed his hair under the cap could have been tawny. He'd become a lawyer and a council member in the upstate town where my mother had grown up. True to his family heritage, he had died young.

"Could it be someone who died before I was born?" I asked.

"Yes, this person could absolutely have *passed over* before you *entered this realm*."

I told her I knew who it was. His name was Joseph.

"Joseph has a very important message for you." Ralph clutched my knee. He was trying not to laugh.

"Joseph wants to tell you that you should trust yourself. Go with your gut. Don't pay any attention to those around you who are trying to control you." She gave me a momlike grin and nodded her head twice.

I squinted at Ralph. The upside of his stolidness was that he thought I was bohemian and exciting. On the other hand, he was a little bossy, about things like talking to other men and no drinking on weeknights.

Later, when I told Ralph about how I thought the message was coming from Grandpa Joseph, he snorted. "What she told you could have applied to anyone."

"No, but there was something about the way she said *tall slim man with light hair*. That's exactly the way my mother always describes him. I mean those exact words, almost. And you know she always says he would have loved to have known his grandchildren. Maybe he's looking out for me."

Another skeptical look, which was at the same time pretty adorable. "Do you want to stop for a salad?"

"At a Thruway rest stop? I mean, I'm not saying I totally believe in it but it's possible. It makes some kind of sense, doesn't it?"

He was getting used to me manufacturing transcendent experiences out of unpromising raw material. "Well, he does sound like someone you could use in your life."

That trip to Lily Dale made me feel that, despite the bossiness, I should move to the city with Ralph like he'd been asking me to do. We had shared a profound or at least otherworldly experience, which tied us to each other.

The point being that I get attached. I got attached to Ralph because of Lily Dale, and I got attached to Jen because of our mutual ambition.

I knew that I should allow in my life only those who valued and nurtured me. But people are like stories, was my experience. Once you've read them, you can't unread them. They're part of your nervous system.

After our conversation, Jen and I had lunch together often. Over vegetable sushi, we talked compulsively about how we could get those jobs.

One night, after one of our intense lunchtime conversations, I went to sleep in a strange state. I got in bed next to my sleeping boyfriend (a new one, not Ralph), and the words Jen repeated like a mantra zapped around in my head: "It all depends on Ted Unden." So did her ambitious soft/hard smile, which sometimes disappeared more quickly than she meant it to, like the opposite of a Cheshire cat. I felt numb, but I imagined something pushing on my numb skin from the inside, like a tumor or an undeveloped twin fetus. I fell asleep right away, as usual. I woke up in the night, which was unusual. I figured I'd use the opportunity to pee. In the bathroom I stared at the mirror. I saw my face I saw my face I saw my face . . . and then I didn't see my face anymore, and I was in another place.

I stood in a flowering wilderness in an infinite space. It seemed to have been laid out with intention, like the great parks of Europe. People were strolling alone or in pairs, so light that their feet hardly skimmed the ground. Others sang in a small chorus or sat quietly with hands folded—an enormous number of people, even an infinite number, but in such an infinite space that it didn't feel crowded. But even though I could see these people, they looked grayed out, inaccessible, and I couldn't make any kind of contact with them. Which was disappointing, because some of the people I saw meant a lot to me, like Pauline Kael and Kurt Cobain and Sojourner Truth. But then I saw that a few of the people in this infinite crowd were in full color and high def and three or maybe even four dimensions. Even if I hadn't recognized them from old family photos, even if I hadn't remembered some of them, my thrill of recognition was instantaneous. These, I knew, were my ancestors.

The first high-def ancestor I saw was Grandpa Joseph, in his business suit, tall, slim and light-haired. I walked quickly to him, wanting a hug, but his arms stayed at his sides. Physical touch didn't seem to be his thing. I understood that: It wasn't my mother's thing either. Instead he said, "You're my little girl's little girl."

"That's right." I looked up into his blue eyes and he looked down into my blue eyes. We were both weeping.

When you're meeting someone for the first time, and you're both weeping with the significance of it, but physical touch isn't an option, what do you do? "Show me where you live," I said, and we walked through the springtime landscape. Everything's heightened in spring—scents, colors, emotions— and spring in the afterworld was more delicately powerful than any I'd ever experienced. It seemed right to be weeping in this beautiful place with a man who had made me but who I'd never known.

And there was Grandma Margaret and Grandpa Frank and Grandma Vincenza and lots of great-aunts and great-uncles and many in the odd clothes of eras even more distant. Some of them I had known briefly as a kid, some were unknown but obviously mine, because they glowed with color and texture and depth. There were also relatives I had known as recently as a few years ago, like Uncle Bob, who had died slowly, crippled and bedridden, of multiple sclerosis. But there he was, playing catch with a grayed-out young man. As Grandpa Joseph clapped him on the back, Uncle Bob leapt into the air and caught the baseball expertly.

He considered me. Did he see that I was someone who needed help making her way through life? "The secret to life is knowing how to forget at any time," he said, "and knowing what to ignore."

So this was how the dead conversed, in blunt, random wisdom moments. I wondered if his wisdom stemmed from his own painful life and death, or whether it was a general truth. Grandpa Joseph and I walked on. I supposed goodbyes were unnecessary in this place beyond death.

We sat down next to a pond. Our time together, we knew, was brief. The hum of the seen but untouchable dead was like the white noise machine my boyfriend needed to go to sleep at night. It was also the soundtrack, slow and fine, to the passage of time.

"Grandpa? I wish I had gotten to know you. I need someone to advise me, a professional person. I need you. Would you be my saint?" I meant guardian angel or intercessor.

He smiled at me, blue eye to blue eye, and now he did hold my hand. "You should listen to your gut. There are people around you who want to control you." I thought at first he was teasing me, but his face was very serious.

Then I was back in the bathroom, bereft.

Not long after, Jen asked me to have drinks with her after work. Ted Unden would be there, "and I think it would be good for him to see you in a social setting."

We went to a bar on 54th Street. The crumbling townhouse had been a workingman's speakeasy in the 1920s (era of Grandpa Joseph's youth) and was now the kind of saloon where men outnumbered women 5 to 1, and men in pressed business shirts outnumbered men in workshirts 100 to 0. Jen, Ted Unden, a few other managers, a few senior creatives, and I sat around a long table. I found myself directly across from Ted, Jen on his right.

Next to me was a woman named Jessica, another junior manager. She made the usual conversational opening.

"I love your bag!"

It was a big sleek orange leather messenger bag. "Oh, thanks! It's from this place on the Lower East Side." My boyfriend had given it to me for my birthday. It was expensive, something I never could have bought for myself.

"It's beautiful," Jessica said. "Where's this place?" I was getting the shop's card out of my wallet when Jen, who'd been laughing with Ted, held up her own bag, patchwork-quilted out of many scraps of bronze, silver, and gold vegan leather. "Wait a minute! I need some attention too!"

She did. I sat back and watched with admiring amusement, like the mother of a precocious, slightly awkward little girl, at her gyrations to capture Ted's attention: the sudden thrustings of various regions of her body, the overlong, overloud laughter at his remarks, the intense nods when he turned serious about business. "The poor thing," I thought.

Soon everyone was drunk and funny. Authors and competitors were trashed with verve. The zingers buzzed around my ears. I listened and laughed, happy to be a good audience member, happy to be included.

"Jesus, he's beyond a joke, he's a tedium."

"So I told him, Go fuck yourself . . . oh wait, you already are."

"She thinks using keep-the-riffraff-out blurbs will win her a National Book Award."

"Get this, no GET THIS, my kid got suspended for bullying. He's gay and he bullied a homophobic, peanut-allergic kid by threatening to shove peanuts down his throat."

After an especially filthy comment about a new bombshell author, Ted Unden turned to me and rolled his eyes in mocking apology. "Hope we're not offending."

"Oh no, it's fine, I. . . ." My voice was too hesitant and soft to be heard in the chaos, and he turned away, on to someone more sure and compelling. I felt timid because he'd misread me. It was an extremely inorganic moment. Jen saw and began telling a story about a movie deal she was trying to close.

Later, when I commented on the author photographer famous for making writers resemble sultry underwear models, saying her subjects all looked like they'd been basted in butter and roasted in a medium-hot oven, I thought maybe I had redeemed myself. . . ?

When we left, I hugged Jen and thanked her again for including me. "You were fine," she said, her smile disappearing, a little tipsy. "Don't worry." Ted Unden whispered something in her ear. She laughed, clasped her shining bag to her chest like a shield, and walked away to the subway arm in arm with Jessica.

That February, Ted Unden said hello to me in the office sometimes. My days were predictable: good, quick, inoffensive work; chats, lunches, and drinks with Jen morning, afternoon, and evening. And a bonus, every so often, unpredictable but always longed for, soothing times with my dead ones at night.

My boyfriend, who wrote code, was absorbed with his own work. He was a self-sufficient person, and my emotional absence didn't seem to bother him. As long as I was available for a couple of dinners a week and sex on Wednesdays and Saturdays, he was happy. (Or I thought he was happy until later that spring, when he told me he was getting back together with his old girlfriend.) So I was available on Wednesdays and Saturdays, but there was often an element of get it over with, because I wanted to sprint to the bathroom mirror, full of hope, and get to that other place.

He was nice though. Sometimes I'd come home and make dinner, and we'd split a bottle of wine. He would sing "Kiss" along with Prince and imitate his smooth moves and make me laugh. My escape-lust would get replaced by the regular kind (and escape from what, anyway?).

We could see a swath of sky outside our bedroom window on the thirtieth floor and we'd cuddle together on Saturdays and on Wednesdays, and watch the sky as if it were a movie screen. "Is it enough to love someone or do you also have to understand them?" I whispered once, and he kissed me, he was a hypnotic kisser, and I forgot what I'd asked. An hour later I was in the bathroom.

After all, I had always craved transcendence, the revelation of eternity behind the flimsy facts of everyday life—lunches, subways, Verizon bills, and working on a relationship. Now I had transcendence in quadruplicate: the dead, the afterworld, unconditional love, and ancient wisdom.

Grandma Vincenza sat on a picnic blanket in a sprigged housecoat, underneath a tree hung with some shining golden fruits. I remembered her soft dark merry eyes from my childhood, when she would tell jokes in Italian and make my aunts laugh. Now they were full of loving amusement. She pulled me onto her cushiony lap and cradled me, a newborn in the world of the dead. I had never, I thought, in the world of the living, felt so at peace.

Jen got busier. When I gave an important presentation, she slipped out in the middle, and she didn't offer to dissect it with me afterwards, which would have been the usual Jen thing to do. "That was. Interesting," was all she said later.

When I asked if there was anything wrong, she laughed. "I didn't realize I had so much power," she said.

After a week of finding her on the phone or staring at her screen whenever I dropped by, I walked into her office to say goodnight. "Let's have drinks," she said. Her hair was unbrushed and there were crumbs on her sweater. It was the most vulnerable I had ever seen her, and in spite of the recent brushoffs it made me want to warm her hands in mine and offer her a soft blanket.

We walked to the vegan place, then past it. We went into the fancy bistro next door, its lights dimmed for the dinner crowd. I ordered wine and she, with a glum look, asked for a festive cocktail, an elderflower martini, garnished with a tiny live white blossom. I asked how her week had been.

"I don't know. I've been thinking about my mother a lot lately. She was... not a very nice person. She wasn't very attractive. She was overweight." I started to jokingly point out that x did not equal y, but she looked so upset that I did take her hand and murmured "Aw, hon, I'm surprised to hear you. . . ."

"I don't know, I've been thinking about her lately. Growing up with her wasn't. . . . She and my father would invite people to our house who she felt could help them in their careers, every single fucking weekend there was a dinner party and every single fucking weekend she would look my sister and me in the eye and say 'We have to impress these people, girls. They're important.' And the people would come and we *would* impress them, you know? By being pretty and polite and charming and interested."

"God, Jen, that sounds oppressive."

"I mean it was just no fun at all. Yeah, oppressive. All those fucking important people. All that striving." She took the blossom out of her cocktail and sucked it. "I wanted to tell you. I knew you'd understand."

My hands went cold then and I untangled from her and checked my phone. When I saw the text from my boyfriend (*r u coming home we nd 2 tlk*), I was too cold to feel surprised.

On my last night in the apartment, I met my other grandmother, Margaret, in the world of the dead. Petite in a dark dress with a white lace collar and heeled orthopedic shoes, this was the woman, my mother had told me, from whom I'd gotten my love of the written word. I had her small clothbound copy of *Jane Eyre*, with her fountain-penned underlinings and notes, on my bookshelf.

I supposed this would be my last visit. The bathroom in my boyfriend's apartment was probably some kind of portal. It was his place. He would hardly miss the quarter of the monthly rent I'd been paying, and it seemed he wouldn't miss the rest of me either. I was going to share a place in Brooklyn with a friend from college.

Grandma Margaret had died when I was six. I remembered her as kind but remote, her roselike face blurred with inwardness.

She smiled now, remotely. If I told her about the breakup, would she care? That sort of thing probably wouldn't matter here. Wherever I looked, alone, connected, or detached, the dead were tranquil.

I held up my right hand to wave hello. She stood facing me and held up her left, in a mirror-gesture. I stepped back with my right foot, she stepped forward with her left. I made an expansive open-armed gesture. So did she. And there we were in a musicless, tranquil mirror-gavotte, like a pair of novice mimes.

A dance with the dead! In the glade dotted with wildflowers, we danced like this for several minutes. Not playful, but full of meaning. But what was the meaning?

I took Grandma Margaret's smooth hand and kissed it. I wanted to stay there with her forever and partake in her nutty remote tranquility. But that was impossible. More than differences between men and women, or managers and creatives, the real division is between the dead and the living.

Finally, she said: "You're in a new place in society now, aren't you? Things are different now than they were twenty-five years ago. Women are just socially in a completely different place now. And I want you to know it's good: You don't have to hate and . . . *slice* each other anymore."

I was baffled. "No, Grandma, I need to talk about love. I mean, my boyfriend just dumped me and I really loved him. I don't know what to do."

"Did you love him enough?" she asked.

I said nothing. It seemed like a question only the dead could ask or answer.

She folded her hands placidly, as if about to make an ultimate pronouncement. I waited for the words that would save me and fix everything.

"Maybe we should truly just care for everyone else by leaving them alone." But wasn't that what I'd done? "But how is that love?"

"Let them grow as they must."

Back in the bathroom, I splashed my face. Then I walked into the living room and finished packing my books.

Some things die suddenly and violently. Some die and allow you to be part of their long process. Then there are the things that seem important and finally reveal themselves as trivial. Also: the things that seem possible and reveal themselves as impossible. Those die when you realize they were never alive.

Jen cornered me in my cubicle on the last day of March.

"Listen. I have something to tell you." She looked me straight in the eye, focused and blank, like a bank officer or the assistant principal in charge of detention. "Ted's decided to give the senior creative job to Jessica. He felt she was further along in terms of author relations and . . . just generally further along."

Jessica had barely been on my radar.

"I know it's tough. I'm encouraging you to look at this as a delay in your goals." Silence. "It doesn't mean. . . ." She couldn't convincingly finish. She told me she would start the management job next month.

"I thought you should know," she said. "I believe in knowledge."

The only appropriate response was "Thank you for telling me."

"I won't be as available to socialize now," she didn't need to say. It would happen organically.

I was about to feel rage and despair about a person who deserved, at best, my irritation. Who meant far far less to me than Grandpa Joseph or Grandma Vincenza or any of them.

I had never understood Jen, I had never tried. People, dead or living, did not yield up their meanings so easily.

Oh my ancestors. I had spent those nights with them and sucked and sucked their ancient wise energy and never once asked them about their lives or their deaths or about the afterlife. Had I visited heaven or hell? Or a different kind of place, beyond judgment, but definitely *other* and *after*? Some Dante I was.

I wasn't sure what to do. Jen stood in front of my desk, very upright but with a veneer of fidgetiness overlaid on her usual poise. She was waiting for my reaction so that she could tell me why I was wrong and then leave.

What I wanted to do was lie down on my side and die. Not in a Sylvia Plath kind of way, because I was too sensitive for this hurtful world, and not in a Dante kind of way, to come back and live better and stronger and wiser with knowledge of the afterworld, but in a Jesus kind of way. I would die to save others. I would lie down on my side and die and green vines and leaves would sprout from every part of me, toes calf knee thigh hipbones crotch navel breasts fingers elbows shoulders neck lips nostrils eye sockets ears and brain. The vines and leaves would grow quickly and abundantly. They would sweeten the air with their exhaled oxygen and their chlorophyll. Like that, I could make up for my failures of empathy and imagination.

Seven years later, when I tried to explain to my toddler the death of her grandmother ("We put her in the ground and now she'll help the flowers grow"), the image wasn't quite as lush or real.

5

On Sadness

I noticed something strange and beautiful about the word "sad." It's the only emotion word that you can use for a general situation and also for how a person feels.

You can say "I'm sad." And when someone dies or love is gone you can say "It's so sad."

You can't say (about a situation) "It's happy" or "It's anxious" or "It's ashamed" or "It's angry."

Sadness seems to be the hardest emotional state to accept and even to honor or celebrate.

I want to leap immediately from "I'm sad" to "The world is ugly and the people are sad."

Or "I'm sad so the world is fucked up so I want to blow up the world."

Or "I'm sad and then it will pass and I'll be happy again."

A. always asked: What do I feel like doing? I always ask: What should I be? Those are two very different ways of being sad

or happy. That's why her death fell like a sea on me. Sadness flopped violently at my feet

then it died too, and now the remnants of sadness lie scattered about the situation, like bones and salt.

The Do-Over

I will not WILL NOT take my authority
to feed my lucky hungers,
nor dub thee "Full of Mourning"
while the sun is loving me.
No aspect of life is to be despised
though we're still sitting cranky in the meadow,
sick, singed, loud and daring.
I see the forest, I see the trees.
What I can't see is the
dappled clearing I'm standing on,
though I know it's deserving
of the pinkest haloes.
To be left with you, big-sky God?
To be a dreamer, overly?
Have I traversed the wood only to go to—No!

My hand is Wyoming, discovered.
It turns the pages of the recent self-help literature
and wherever I look there are faces like sunbeams.

So kiss the mainstream culture, let it go.

Let go of that beautiful despair.
The shackles of the lyric, let them go.
In the clearing, the *now* is falling.
We clean ourselves,
preserve our sanity by playing,
work quickly with fine impulses.
The color of what we choose turns into a remedy,
an important minor sacrament.
There's something modern within us,
grieving in middle age,
and its intensity stands
between us and death

in the school, the dappled school, of patience.

A. *in September*

A piece of you flew into me one day, a
Niggling hooked little finger of spirit. I was
Driving. It didn't hurt, it tickled.
Randomly, I'd been wondering how to become a baby cuddler.
Even though I didn't have a baby anymore, I could substitute.
After all, lots of hospitals must need cuddlers.

Forget it, I thought immediately. It wouldn't be the same.
Oh! It tickled when I knew it would never be the same and I
Remembered suggesting it to you once, when you were
Sad there were no more babies in your life, no
Toddlers, your grandchildren were tweens now—
Except you didn't like the idea. You wanted a connection you couldn't
Really get from a scheduled cuddle with an unrelated baby,

Only from an impossible baby of your own.
So you had limitations too. What you taught me:
Screw limitations. Love anyway, and hard.
I remembered this when it flew, the
Piece in me of you.

Words for a Newborn

Little craftier than you are,
        every day in every part of the world
                people set out to teach

something to others or to study
        something themselves.
                This increases the likelihood that

        desired actions will occur,
but only if the performance

is a *possible* performance.
        You know already that participation
                doesn't always equalize power.

There is much disagreement
        about the importance of you,
                whether the ritual attraction we feel

for you is a sexual bureaucracy
        or a function of good light,
                oh yellow indeterminate sprout.

We don't know how to grasp
        your extreme flexibility,
                nor your ultimate time-stamp.

You'll learn many procedures
        for mastering everyday life. You'll learn
                to think like a computer and like a plant,

        finding a choice unnecessary.
You'll learn not to reduce people to things.

We resist giving advice, we ourselves
        have messed up so often. We resist too
                the platitude that *all* is possible.

Listen: At times you may have a demon
        that forces its way up. Will you grow
                tentative of future connection?

        Or trust the likeness between yourself
and daylilies trim and brash in the field?

Power situations are not creative;
        flowers no freer than we are;
                you'll give yourself to every fresh chaos until

you sort the array into mind-sized bites.
        This performance will fill eighty years
                or more. We wish you

        innocence, strength, promise, and surrender,
a gradual and natural growth.

The Arrival of Spring

(Botticelli)

"So then you were. . . ."
"So then I was *what?*"
And the whole seabeach

just beyond the trees
widens. Italian? Blonde?
Charming? In a

scarcity economy,
kindness is bread,
and if kindness comes

from lust, so be it.
A bubbly state of
monumental

opportunity has left
every gal a
little bit pregnant,

while every guy
hangs around the edges,
stirring the shit.

And yet, they aren't
heinous, an oldtime
ardor prevails.

Of course we are
endlessly
fascinating to ourselves.

What you did for me,
what I did for you,
masters the world

with brave
dark injury,
afterwards sitting

criss-cross-applesauce
on the meadow floor.
And even when

mastered,
broken,
we

feel pleasantly free.
Love triumphs
over brutality

because brutality
must end
with death, and love

never does, it
can always
find a new

sky or a
sheepdog,
and we believe

this because
it's our job to
believe it,

and if you can't
believe it perhaps
you need a harder

kick in the ass
or whispered
admiration

delivered in a
loose slurred voice.
Notice, please,

the freshness,
the tang that says
the only thing

to do is keep
working. Master
the same world,

please, with petite
licks of ecstasy.
Remember, the

sweat weather
is months away.
Beneath the cult,

a baroque mystery,
mischievous and
sans pain.

Under the feet,
the splaying myrtle.
Around the pretty

faces, the year's first
no-see-ums.
Below the canopy,

all is explained,
everything's
explainable
and explained.

Funeral of My Character

(paintings by Hikari Shimoda)

What is lost is lost for good reason. Things turn bizarre when the canvas of my feelings is better off in front of the MacBook at home.

Night may tell why every day is bigger and more worth knowing.

Morning may find me rereading the quote on the tea mug.

Afternoon may pose questions like whether I need to put on a bra and wash my face for the babysitter

while twilight sees me as Yoko Ono, superior, isolate, intrusive and revered.

Similarly, months pass. A bodybuilder can never be mistaken for anything but a bodybuilder. But a sensitive type is, in June, sufficiently unmedicated and high on the (gosh) golden light.

In February I see the first wildflower peep from under the snow. It waves to me on its stem.

When summer is done, I watch the stem crack, bend over, get brown and stiff. But that's all right. Because I know the seed will live under the snow.

Similarly, at the funeral of my character, I undergo an (ouch) translation. My character is built up and scraped away like acrylic on a canvas.

My character tells me: A moral or an ending is a lie; but a story that can't end is incomplete

and is waiting for someone to finish it, in the simplest manner possible.

One Short Lyric

Expectation lingers
just like a memory.

Oh, wow, mausoleums,

says the man who doesn't remind me of you

except that everything reminds me of you, except mausoleums.

In the important world (my imagination), I am watching you, simply, without hope or dream. In the unimportant world, this man and I are driving past the cemetery.

The mausoleums *are* impressive, ornate. They seem meant to crumble, suddenly and violently, like the class system, but they have not, and it has not. The angels that guard them are elegant, Edwardian,

hard, cold and unemotional. Their expressions won't change

except to be wiped away, very gently, by time. They are what I now want to be. They never utter the sentence I utter most frequently:

"I do but I don't."

There's nothing good about ill-timed death. Nor about the death of love. That poetry glamorizes them disturbs me. I don't want to be lying in that cemetery. I don't want to be sitting in the cemetery

on a stone bench, thinking about others. I don't want to be sitting in this car, on a bucket seat of hot plush, with the man who gets excited by mausoleums.

There's no fooling the sweet dumb pulse.

Your heart chalks a chair, I sit down.

Borrowings

Weldon Kees, "For My Daughter"; *David Blaine: Street Magic*; Sylvia Plath, "The Moon and the Yew Tree"; Wislawa Szymborska, "Negative"; John Le Carré, *Tinker Sailor Soldier Spy*; *Fortunes of War* (1987 BBC miniseries); Sylvia Plath, "Mirror"; Gertrude Stein, "Four Saints in Three Acts"; Philippe Ariès, *The Hour of Our Death*; anonymous posts on datalounge.com; Whoopi Goldberg's voiceover for the Hayden Planetarium's *Journey to the Stars*; *Ecclesiastes* 9:10; Elizabeth Bishop, "One Art"; Wallace Stevens, "Gubbinal"; Poetry CreatOR 2; Tracy Kidder, *The Soul of a New Machine*; *Best in Children's Books* (Doubleday, 1959); Emily Dickinson, "Because I could not stop for Death."

Mike Ricca

KATHLEEN OSSIP is the author of *The Cold War* (one of *Publishers Weekly's* Best Books of 2011), *The Search Engine* (selected by Derek Walcott for the American Poetry Review/Honickman First Book Prize), and *Cinephrastics*, a chapbook of movie poems. Her poems have appeared in *The Best American Poetry*, *The Paris Review*, *American Poetry Review*, *Boston Review*, *The Washington Post*, *The Believer*, *A Public Space*, and *Poetry Review* (London). She teaches at The New School in New York and online for The Poetry School of London. She was a founding editor of *LIT* and is the poetry editor of *Women's Studies Quarterly*. She has received a fellowship from the New York Foundation for the Arts.